A Rational Advance for the Labour Party

John
LLOYD

A Rational Advance for the Labour Party

Chatto & Windus
LONDON

Published in 1989 by
Chatto & Windus Ltd
30 Bedford Square
London WC1B 3SG

A CIP catalogue record for this book
is available from the British Library

ISBN 0 7011 3519 0

Photoset in Linotron Ehrhardt by
Rowland Phototypesetting Ltd
Bury St Edmunds, Suffolk
Printed in Great Britain by
Redwood Burn Ltd
Trowbridge, Wiltshire

LABOUR IS the foundation of the politics which will replace conservatism. Saved from spinning into irrelevance at considerable effort, it has – now, in 1989, for the first time in a decade – the potential to propose electoral and governing strategies which could not only win power but, more importantly, revive democratic and collective practices which have atrophied.

The policies of Labour need to be made explicit. They will be social democratic: that is, they will be sharply distinguished both from free-market neo-liberalism which allocates no place to democratic politics beyond periodic electoral contests, and, much more sharply, from extreme visions or realities of socialism which put politics in charge of everything and allow little or no choice. They will fully accept competitive markets in goods and services, while developing a framework within which much more effective collective actions may be shaped, and the asocial effects of markets constrained.

Labour came from traditions of struggle for democratic expression; of self-organisation for collective protection and advancement; of cooperation across national boundaries for peaceful development and assistance. It can only be true to itself if it draws on that past. It can only be true to its past if it reshapes it for the present and future rather than – as it has done – allow past structures to become monuments.

We have seen, in the past decade, neo-conservatism find in some of its 18th and 19th century intellectual roots a new source of strength. Labour's traditions were in part born of the struggle against the consequences of these free market doctrines in practice: they were rooted in, though never exclusive to, the class formed by industrial capitalism – the working class.

As the nature of markets and of capital has changed, so has the sociology of the workforce. The division of labour is international; workers are diverse, fragmented, not to be mobilised in huge aggregations for political or any other purposes. They have, more often than not, more power as consumers, more time and discrimination. None of this means – as it has been interpreted as meaning – that their need or taste for new democratic forms and for collective projects is exhausted or surpassed by the demands of consumption. It does mean that these forms and projects must spring from the conditions and meanings of their life and not be extruded upon it from a past which dogmatists and sentimentalists refuse to reinterpret.

Both internal, organisational change (with which I deal in the next section) and developments in domestic and international politics will make this new response possible. In brief, the task is to

– provide a framework for collective efforts that involve the citizenry in social and economic life and that give the principle of citizenship real meaning, rather than the rhetorical one it has so far acquired;

– democratise our constitution and institutions in ways which facilitate the expression of political choice and which give transparency to the political process

– revive, in new forms, a sense of social cohesion through the development of reciprocal rights and responsibilities

– take advantage of an unusually hopeful trend in international relations at a time when the interdependence of the world has been borne home to all, and when the barriers to good East–West relations are swiftly diminishing.

We cannot escape from the fact that socialism has been corrupted: corrupted most of all by totalitarian states of the East, where a Marxist-Leninist revolution inscribed terror, then authoritarian centralism, in the politics of the Soviet Union and later in the politics of the states which came under its hegemony. The vigour with which this past is now being revised within the Soviet Union and some of the East European states has a huge significance –

most of all, of course, for these states themselves. For Western socialists, the exercise has a different importance: it reveals to us again, how precious the traditions of democracy, liberalism and gradualism have been and are; it allows us to frame our policies with a more robust care for the freedoms which the revisionists of the East are now beginning to discover for themselves. It helps us, in short, to determine what we must not do.

We must not attempt to cut hard against the grain of our societies' development. As citizens become more empowered by knowledge and by wealth, as they become more diffuse in their tastes and their cultures, domestic politics becomes, willy nilly, more and more of a ring-holding operation within which forces in civil society struggle and cooperate. Naturally, it is a fundamental *political* choice which framework one constructs for these forces. The framework we construct must accept economic freedom and competition because we know now, from our own and others' experiences, how bad the all-powerful state can be in this field – the worse, the more heavily it is present. But the framework must also stimulate and give space to the groups and organisations in which our society is rich, and with which government must increasingly learn to share power and responsibility. It is to this plurality that social democracy must look, to find the springs of its *own* revival.

Cutting with the grain can be interpreted as mere quietism. It is not that. 'Thatcherism' – not a quietist movement – read the prevailing forces in the seventies and eighties accurately, and shaped its politics to accommodate them (indeed, these forces are often what people actually mean when they talk of 'Thatcherism'). They included: global interdependence, the internationalisation of production and of markets, the boom in consumption and the consumer ethic, the collapse of communism's moral and ideological authority (and the concomitant bolstering of that of the free market), the blurring of the configurations of class and the loss of its political potency, at least for the left.

Many of these movements, in which Britain has played a minor part or even been merely a spectator, do indeed favour a politics of the right rather than the left. At the least, they have presented the parties of the left with a more difficult political task, since more of their baggage had to be jettisoned to allow them to ride, rather than be swamped by, these tides (which has not prevented the Australian, French, Italian, New Zealand, Norwegian, Swedish and Spanish socialist or labour parties from doing just that).

But there is nothing deterministic about all of this. Interdependence and internationalisation were – are – reflexes of the left more than of the right. The steady growth in the size and power of transnational companies, which is the largest feature of internationalisation, calls for the steady development of countervailing power – another cause for the left. Popular consumption and taste have been championed and influenced before by socialists and social democracy has never directed its appeal solely to one class, even if its narrower adherents would wish it to. Finally, the impasse in which state communism finds itself can best be addressed – in the view of many of the reformists in communist societies – by a socialist politics which encourages free market efficiency but does not give up on one of these societies' real achievements – full employment.

Neither time nor chance has passed the Labour Party by – provided it redefines its purpose and practice. A politics whose instincts and tradition incline it towards the collective, which sees individuals as meaningless without their societies, which seeks to give secular and material expression to the charitable insights of religion, certainly has a place – which can again be a politically dominant one – in what may already be seen of the future. Such a place awaits a party for whom the freedom of individuals is set off by the responsibilities we must constantly assume in freedom's name.

And spurn the dust, to win the prize

There should be no pretence that a Labour victory is likely at the next election – even if, as this essay is written, Labour now level-pegs with the Government in some polls. Further, we should make it clear that it is not desirable for the country that *any* party 'wins' by means of the present electoral system, though of course Labour will have to use it at least one more time in order to gain power and usher in its own reform.

Labour – the point is argued below – must not call for a change in the electoral system merely because it can no longer win on the present one. It must argue for a more proportional, and thus more democratic system, because it has accepted that the more pluralistic society described above will wish for more political as well as every other kind of choice; and because it must demonstrate that it is willing to share power with representatives of other traditions.

Labour must also demonstrate that it no longer relies on mobilising blocks of 'tied' votes (trade unionist or public sector dwellers and employees) but that instead, it recognises the need to formulate progressive policies with a cross-class appeal based on their rational response to the current situation.

This will mean, not necessarily pacts (though there will be circumstances in which a pact might be appropriate), but certainly a public discussion with other opposition about common purposes – especially the common purpose to amend the electoral system. Labour will lead in such a forum, as David Owen at least has already recognised. But it will not lead by assuming that it is a monopolist of the opposition coming once again into its own.

There is no reason why this process should not be successfully undertaken by a party with Neil Kinnock as its head. This needs perhaps less arguing now than it has done for much of the period since the last election, but it is still, I would judge, sufficiently striking to need some underpinning for many, especially for those of the intelligentsia who have expressed their contempt for him. My view is that this contempt can often say more about the introversion and sense of political futility suffered by much of the left intelligentsia than about Kinnock; but there has been rational cause for it too. To explain this, however, requires a historical detour.

Though the left was the engine driving Labour into irrelevance in the late seventies and early eighties, the main responsibility for its internal collapse lay with a right wing which was in the ascendancy in the parliamentary party and yet very largely threw in the towel or attempted to compromise where no compromise was actually available. Since the right did not take on board the seriousness and depth of the left assault, and thus did not fight it with a seriousness and depth of its own, it is illogical to charge those who led the fraction which became the Social Democrats with treachery or cowardice. Had they stayed to help lead the right side in the fratricidal struggle within the party they might, ultimately, have beaten the left to win the policies which have since been adopted. (However, they can argue that their defection produced these policies faster, and the fact of such a struggle would have certainly still meant the rise of the centre and the continuing retention of power by the Conservatives.)

What, after all, did they choose to leave? A party whose every facet – organisation, policy, membership – saw the left gaining ground with the overt participation of organised Trotskyist groups. Party life, in many areas of the country, was either inert or dogmatic, or dogmatically inert. Membership was falling, especially among working class members. The policy slid towards a programme in which few of the leading figures believed. The unions, whose party 'membership' of millions were phantoms and which were themselves increasingly zealot-ised, were regarded as the long-stop – for cash, votes and sense. Socially, the party was intolerant and suspicious; organisationally, it was overstretched and formalistic; politically, it was inchoate.

The left had huge enthusiasm and energy in pursuit of their policy goals – complete nationalisation of the corporate sector and banking, unilateral renunciation of nuclear weapons, withdrawal from Nato, sexual and racial separatism, inner party constitutional change to secure democratic centralism and the huge extension of trade union power. The centre and right (the difference was more social than political) by contrast, simply refused to renew itself politically. To sigh that Tony Crosland had died was hardly an alibi. There *were* a number of parliamentary and extra-parliamentary figures able to think through a social democratic programme, difficult as the decisions consequent upon that exercise would have been. Instead, a holding operation was mounted which sought to defuse both left wing and trade union demands by proposing an ever more complex corporatism. This would have had to draw on reservoirs of expertise which the unions did not have and would not develop – and enthusiasm which the employers did not have and would not develop. In the 1979–83 period, policy formation became rather fantastical: that is to say, the proposals and plans largely lost touch with any kind of social or industrial base, and thus lost the votes both of the centre-left middle classes and of that part of the working class which benefited from 'Thatcherite' industrial restructuring.

Thus the left's charge that the 1974–79 Governments had 'sold out' socialism had the field within the party pretty much to itself. That view was made much more potent by being championed by Tony Benn, then the most energetic and charismatic figure in the Labour Party, who had the added authority of having seen the sell-out from the inside of the Cabinet room.

Of course, those Governments *did* fail; not in the sense of failing to set in place the worker-controlled siege economy which (in some versions) the left called for – they did not do so but that was never their intention – but in the sense of failing to develop a functioning social democracy in which the state, labour and capital could broadly agree priorities, powers, trade-offs and responsibilities. The social contract, which was surely seen as that, at least in embryo, had limited if important success in bringing down inflation and protecting the most vulnerable members of society. However, it did not attempt to grapple with the fact that the Government's two social partners were manifestly unfitted for the corporate roles assigned to them, since neither could nor would deliver on centrally-agreed deals over a sustained period. Nor were they encouraged to. The shibboleth of free collective bargaining, that divisive and arbitrary system to which the majority of trade unions cleaved, was said to be temporarily suspended pending repairs, after which the free-for-all (where unions would of course be part of the 'all') would again begin.

The failure of interventionism/corporatism when in power was followed by the adumbration of an extreme social liberalism in opposition: I mean by that the very great salience given to sexual rights, to anti-racism and to at least an implicit critique of much routine working class and middle class social behaviour. Much of this outraged those who behaved in this way, especially if they thought their children were being educated to behave or think differently. Further, an all-out and successful assault on the retention of the British nuclear deterrent – this supported wholeheartedly by the post-Callaghan party leadership – succeeded in making the Party unilateralist. Finally, the considerable hostility to the European Community located largely in the Party's left but with pockets of support elsewhere, also won the policy day. The Party to whose leadership Neil Kinnock succeeded in October 1983 was, in formal terms, for a socialist siege economy when the world was becoming rapidly more economically intertwined and when UK trade flows were increasingly with other EC members; it was for unilateralism while the Soviet Union remained monolithically impervious to change and militarily preponderant in Europe; it was for the extremes of liberalism while public morality was tending to be rather conservative. No wonder that academic psephologists and political scientists now conclude, in the main, that it is *political* rather than demographic reasons which must be held responsible for Labour's loss of support.

In the six years since then, the Kinnock leadership

a) has marginalised the far left
b) has pushed up Labour's share in the polls from 27 per cent in the 1983 election to 32 per cent in 1987 and 40 per cent in the most recent opinion polls.
c) has begun the move away from trade union domination of conference and thus of policy
d) has achieved the acceptance of social democratic principles as the basis for policy
e) has joined the mainstream of the European left in its enthusiasm for a more united and more 'social' Europe
f) is likely to move away from its unilateralist posture. Kinnock already has.

These are large and solid achievements. They are the more so for having been accomplished while Kinnock fought against his *own* grain, his *own* reflexes – the traits which had made *him* the most popular fellow in the Labour Party – fashioning a determined social democrat out of the clay of a left-wing neo-Bevanite. Kinnock has grasped what other successful European socialist leaders such as François Mitterand, Felipe Gonzales and Benito Craxi have: first get control of the Party – no matter how long it takes – for if you cannot control the party, nothing else can be accomplished. His struggle has been long and he has had to go for his objectives in a crab-wise fashion. But the rot was deep and the party's structure, in particular its fatal reliance on the union block vote, was very resistant to change.

He is not an intellectual, nor an economist. He has had to learn to rely on senior colleagues whose particular talents are greater than his – and he is fortunate in having many who are talented. His self-remoulding has been at the expense of his affability, which has been replaced by a certain abrasiveness and a tendency, now said to be corrected, to isolate himself from advice and contrary opinion. But that he has been effective cannot be doubted: that he has assumed the crushing responsibilities of Labour leadership is clear. He has changed and led his party through change, which neither he nor it thought possible, or at one time desirable. There is an argument which concedes him his successes but holds that his limitations make him unelectable and that he should therefore step down with the gratitude of all, in favour of John Smith or possibly Bryan Gould. He is unlikely to see much merit in this argument and unless the party barons show greater resolve than they did in the much more extreme case of Michael Foot, he will not be pushed. Besides, he has it in his power to prove his critics wrong. He has the vigour, intelligence and skill. And he has colleagues who have the same qualities in as much measure as their Government opposites.

That he has not yet done enough is an index of the distance which Labour had put between itself and rational politics, *and* of the swiftness with which politics itself has moved. The Policy Review has been over-timid and bureaucratic in its conception. The union ties remain too strong, and will remain so for too long. Though it *is* likely that unilateralism will go, it may do so by means of a compromise which does not exist except verbally. It will be extremely difficult to renew party life in many areas to the point where people can join with the expectation both of comradeship and of purposeful activity.

Yet what has been done is enough to render the Party fit for a new period in its history: one in which its conscious purpose is the creation of a social democratic programme and political style which rest on the domestic pillar of democracy and reciprocal responsibility, and the international pillar of interdependence. In seeking the political mechanisms by which these great themes can work their way out in practice, Labour can – if it grasps the chance – both command and inspire.

. . . Unites the human race

An obvious fact is also an important one: the post-war period has been, for the war's combatants and for other countries too, a period of unparalleled prosperity and relatively free political and social development (the two have by no means always walked hand in hand). The Western imperial powers have given up their empires. Only the Soviet Union could be said to have acquired and kept satellites towards which they behaved as colonial masters – a tutelage which, in the Gorbachev period, is probably being lifted and, in Eastern Europe, may already have been. The advanced capitalist and state socialist countries all experienced more or less strong economic growth throughout the post-war period. That growth slowed in the 1970s – though not for the newly industrialising countries, which could and did take advantage of US and Euro-sclerosis. Within the OECD camp, the advanced capitalist nations which had been the main protagonists in two 'world' wars developed a system of cooperation and negotiation which constantly and routinely smoothed down tensions between them to manageable and non-critical levels.

These real advances co-exist with the persistence

and deepening of miserable poverty, especially in Africa, Asia, and large parts of Latin America. The inequalities of wealth within the advanced economies are as nothing to the inequalities within the poorer countries of the world. Such inequalities occur more frequently in countries where human liberties are violated. In too many states, freedom from such oppression is a long way off. In South Africa, the tyranny of the whites has shifted and sought to liberalise, but it remains a tyranny presently too powerful and too fearful to be dislodged. In the Middle East, Lebanon is the ruins of a state; while the Palestinian leadership has flagged up an ambiguous if promising commitment to recognise the state of Israel, Israel itself remains embattled and intransigent and the Palestinians remain stateless. This is not the best of possible worlds.

Nonetheless, we have come to a crucial juncture in world politics. The interdependence of nations and the fact that the world's most powerful states – the US, Japan, Western Europe, the Soviet Union, China – now speak of being able, not just to avoid war among themselves, but actually to develop co-operative relations, is a wholly momentous development which we have not yet taken on board. Perhaps this is because we cannot quite yet believe it – and rightly so – we should give it time before we do. We now have the possibility of focusing energy and wealth precisely on what is remediable in the world's horrors – both those which we can see about us, like poverty, and those which we know will come, like ecological disaster. Interdependence, the product of those deeply unpopular things, rootless capital and nuclear weapons, has given us the largest of possibilities, only dreamed of by the most utopian of socialists.

Capital is now homeless and entirely mobile: the financial markets are global and instantaneous. The power and reach of the markets now permit – command – much larger takeovers and mergers, a trend that is encouraged by the approach of the single European market. The rapid technical innovations in production technology and systems, in communications and in electronic and other consumer goods, mean that any states seeking to offer their citizens a modern, secular definition of the good life – and how many have been able to withstand that, since the vision of it is so easily available through the media? – must adopt these advances more or less immediately. Development 'independent' of these forces has been possible but at an escalating social and political cost, as the communist countries now show. Their failure to fashion an alternative system which can rival the capitalist one in power has been the largest impetus behind the reform leadership in the USSR and China.

Naturally, the very dynamism of the forces of capital and technology favours and reinforces the already strong: the primary commodity producers of the third world, hopelessly indebted, have for a decade seen both their relative and their absolute poverty grow and deepen as a direct consequence of deflation by the advanced nations. Yet binding the commodity producers so firmly and so all-inclusively into a one-market system has also raised the spectre of their awful poverty to haunt our consciences. It is the task of pure market politics to suppress that ghost. It is the task of socialist politics to exorcise it by addressing its torment.

Less comprehensive in its scope than capital, but tighter in the bonds it wraps about the protagonists, is the mutual ability of the Nato Alliance (640m people) and the Warsaw Pact (400m people) to annihilate each other. This state of routinised terror has perhaps kept peace between two blocs who might otherwise have given each other cause for war through conventional means. But whether or not that is the case is beside the present point – which is that the military-technological competition between the two pacts can no longer be afforded if their consumption standards are not to suffer increasingly. This fact, much more stark in the Soviet Union than in the West, has largely forced a change in Soviet foreign policy which in turn is the largest factor in the hoped-for transformation of the international environment. For the first time since the race began, the malign and complex knot which binds our societies at least as closely as bonds of friendship is being tugged at seriously, rather than for effect.

Finally, Western Europeans are engaged in the unique enterprise of building a political, economic and social union between independent states without the use of force or the threat of invasion. That such a project can even be contemplated is extraordinary – we British have not made much of that – *and* puts flesh on some half-forgotten socialist idealism. The vision of the Community, adumbrated by its President, Jacques Delors, as a space within which efficiency and greater wealth can be pursued *at the same time as* workers' rights and social provision are improved, strikes many in Britain as odd, since it is an axiom of our Government that the two have a zero sum rather than a complementary relationship. But so much the better for Labour.

Over the past decade, the reports of three UN Commissions, each chaired by a prominent social democratic politician, have identified common European aims in north–south relations, in security and in the environment. The Brandt, Palme and Brundtland Reports each dwell on the *interconnectedness* of our world: on the impossibility of any major national action being taken without international consequences. Each presents a challenge to the will and responsibility of governments and individuals. Each report points up the need for, and the possibilities of, the meshing of national priorities with international ones. Each report argues for the conscious shaping of programmes which will reduce tension, debt and pollution and become part of the normal political process.

This is not a complete departure from post-war practice: rather you can say it is a *realisation* of it anew, at a higher level and with the added impetus which a less divided world now presents to us. The division of the capitalist and socialist worlds into antagonistic power blocs was not just an irrational and jingoistic matter largely arranged for the benefit of arms manufacturers: both sides had deeply conflicting geopolitical interests, while the Soviet side possessed, until very recently, an explicitly imperialist ideology. In such circumstances, it is hard to resist the conclusion that an armed stasis was the best fearful human beings could manage.

Now we have a real chance to manage something better. As this is written, at the beginning of 1989, many theatres of conflict or tension show actual or putative signs of improvement, several of these as a direct consequence of the shift in Soviet policy (a demonstration of what a barrier that policy was). Thus far, the policy continues to develop in a way which seems to indicate it can be trusted: if this continues, it will throw the onus on the *right* to produce a response which is more than a nostalgia for the Cold War.

Within these spaces now created, a Labour foreign policy can be constructed. It will not be – cannot be – a 'socialist foreign policy' of the kind our rhetoric threw up in the last decade, full of abstractly dogmatic schemes for rearranging the world, or at least our place in it. We start from where we are: we preserve and deepen the co-operation among our allies; we make the largest efforts to support and exploit the opportunities created by the reformist Soviet leadership; we try to encourage the foreign policy of the advanced states further in the direction of cooperative projects that safeguard the environment, and help the impoverished nations. Through conscious efforts, through the continuing increase in our wealth, through technical advance, we are able to make what has been socialist utopianism something of a reality.

Most urgently, Labour must establish two (practical) principles at the very heart of its foreign policy. One is furthering, through *negotiation* and *agreement*, the reduction of nuclear armaments. It is clear that British traditions and culture do not allow for a disarmament process that is not clearly seen by the public as reciprocal. It is clear that the two great alliances require relative stability within their own ranks to present each to the other as a negotiating partner. It is of course the task of British politicians to continue to put before the electorate the fact that

British power is no longer great and to draw certain defence expenditure conclusions from that – something which the Conservative Government has baulked at doing. It is no less their duty to recognise the importance of the UK within the Nato alliance and within disarmament negotiations, and to use this weight within Nato to argue for phased and reciprocal disarmament. This is a responsibility Labour has shrunk from enshrining in policy, under pressure from an idealist unilateralism within its ranks that is rightly unshared by the majority of the voters.

There is no fudge available between unilateralism and multilateralism, as the unilateralists on-the-run now suggest. But to be actively in pursuit of agreements to reduce tension and thus stockpiles is a position not presently occupied in British politics. To occupy it would assist both the Party and, more importantly, the disarmament process.

The second principle is this: Britain is part of Europe and is thus part of the unifying process. The old anti-European whingeing – that Europe is a 'rich man's club', that it would undercut a socialist strategy for national economic regeneration and that it is both overly bureaucratic *and* laissez-faire – carries on a ghostly after-life largely confined to the British Labour Group Old Believers in the Strasbourg Parliament and the Brussels Berlaymont. Labour has the chance to renew its politics by embracing a principle which socialists, social democrats and indeed Christian Democrats in the other member states largely accept: that the construction of new social traditions and networks has to be the objective of programmes active at every political level, if the newly unified market is not to fall prey to regional and social tensions.

Why should Labour claim a more effective and coherent vision than the Government *here* – in an area from which it has sometimes seemed, almost perversely, to absent itself? For two reasons: first, because its policy reorientation has the great merit of allowing it to come at the international scene with fresh eyes and with an urgent commitment to build on all that is new and hopeful; second and more importantly, because the new opportunities favour collective and cooperative responses, responses which are native to Labour and its traditions. There is no other political party in Britain which can give the necessary force to that sort of politics. It is Labour's responsibility and its opportunity to do so.

. . . ends the age of cant

Labour has uttered its share of cant about markets, to the point where it seemed at one time to be wholly against them – even, in extreme cases, to be against consumption as an enjoyable activity in itself. These political and cultural attitudes were distasteful to a large body of people who enjoyed rising living standards and the spending of that increased income on commodities.

It cannot be reasonably denied that markets which offer large choice enhance democracy at an everyday – that is, the most commonly felt and pervasive – level. To be able to choose between goods and services is to exercise power of an important and immediate kind; it was distressing to see a party which rightly makes much of the horrors of poverty be so niggardly over the joys of mass consumption. Anyone who doubts how much choice and plenty raises living standards need only compare shopping in Glasgow with shopping in Gorki.

Capitalist production and the free market have produced both choice and plenty in the advanced industrial states. Since the only available large scale alternative has not, and no putative third way is immediately available, it makes sense (indeed there is little choice but) to frame a politics which recognises and works with this sphere – and which encourages it to produce more and better choices. Naturally, in the case of the UK, the foreign consumer is at least as important as the domestic one – a fact only partially recognised in practice even now.

The point for Labour is not to seek to suppress

the market (it no longer does) but to recognise its boundaries and limitations for a politics which is in business to advance the area of democracy. Good at providing choice in goods and services, the market and market principles cannot define democracy, nor can they guarantee it. Where the Government talks cant is in its claim to have captured the high ground of democracy and liberty by 'setting the people free' from, among other institutions, elected authorities. But such freedom is merely a removal of processes of accountability which may have been sclerotic or corrupt, but still constituted the forums and checks of a civil society. The freedom to be relatively or completely hedonistic is not, in the long run, a freedom which can be sustained. The choices which a properly working market confers need to be complemented not just by political pluralism, but by a continually nurtured civic process which promotes and develops the *political* to complement the *material* choice.

There is a powerfully articulated view, strongly run by neo-liberals and immensely supportive to the style of the present Government, which holds that, following periodic markings of crosses on ballot papers, the vast bulk of people wish merely to be left alone, to enjoy private pursuits while a competent, and of course occasionally accountable government, acts in their name; any alternative brings into play activists, committees and delays.

This cannot really hold up. The Government has itself proposed the figure of the 'active citizen' – largely as a recognisably individualist alternative to the collective mechanisms of welfarism, partly as an antidote to (or a placebo for) increasing crime. As Michael Ignatieff put it in *Political Quarterly* (Jan–March 1989), the figure is a 'good-hearted, property-owning patriot, who serves as an unpaid JP if asked, does jury service, gives a day a week to meals on wheels, checks that the old age pensioner next door is tucked up on cold days, and so on'. Nothing wrong with such a person as far as the vision goes, but it is deliberately curtailed.

The most obvious limitation is that while the citizen does more than mind his own business, he extends himself only into the business of his neighbours and of objects of charity. It is, at least in rhetoric, the replacement of bureaucratic provision by human kindness and civic concern.

It is perfectly decent but wholly inadequate. The fragmentation of social life by both private and public development, the hugely complex patterns of work in any urban street, the privatisation of entertainment and leisure, the flight of the middle classes from 'bad' areas, and of their children from these areas' schools, mean that the cosy version of community within which the active citizen is presumed to operate has less and less of a real existence. The more community is invoked (by both right and left), the more elusive it becomes.

The removal of, for example, utilities from public ownership does not remove them from the public sphere, particularly when they are absolute or near-monopolies. All of the services which are piped, cabled or transmitted into our homes are rightly felt to raise issues of pricing, safety, efficiency and morality which can only be settled in the public arena. The rapid growth of corporate size and power is no more a matter solely to be dealt with by market principles than the public sector is. In truth, corporations are willy nilly 'public' (in the civil rather than the commercial sense) as well. They are providers of commodities and of jobs; they dictate education standards, affect retirement assumptions, demand transport and other infrastructure, exercise demographic pressures, confer and destroy status. Their pricing, wage and investment decisions are a major determinant of the country's economy. To regard them, as the Government affects to do, as agents wholly independent of and largely untrammelled by the state is a fiction.

Less than in most other democratic countries are the policies and decisions of corporations in Britain open to their workers. Labour must bear some blame: the attempts to introduce industrial democracy in the mid 1970s fell victim as much to trade union sectionalism as to the fierce opposition of the employers. Labour's anti-EEC stance prevented it, until recently, from grasping the advances which continental traditions and practices could usher in here.

The sphere of largely publicly funded and provided services – health, education and social services – suffers not only from underfunding but from a legacy, longer than this past decade, of denying clients any means of control or even redress. This has not everywhere been seen to be a fatal weakness: the health service, in large part, is strongly supported because its core concept – good provision, largely egalitarian and free at point of use – has been so robust, at least until now. In the cases of education and the social services however, it has become clearer that the lack of effective elective control, and the failure to involve the clients of the services in the formulation of service standards, is a large democratic gap which weakens the legitimacy of public provision itself.

Shorn of a structure within which to act, the putative active citizen will find his or her impulses at once stimulated and straitjacketed. Further, insofar as there is a response to the call for citizens to be active, it will (as free markets do) favour the already well endowed – the articulate, relatively leisured and organisationally skilled. To repeat the point: it would be an excellent thing if such people did take a more active part in charitable and civic activities, but their doing so does not constitute a *citizenry* engaged, or re-engaged, in *citizenship*.

The only political groupings which could lead a renaissance of citizenship are those on the political left with the Labour Party as the inevitable major partner. I return below to Labour's and the other parties' responsibilities in a period where it is as sure as political forecasting can make it, that none can win power unaided or un-pacted: here the opposition parties are bracketed together to point up that the traditions of all of them mesh with a real rather than a cosmetic form of citizenship. The real thing must be inclusive and must enable – through open institutions which are elective and have authority – the participation of all.

How? Through elective education and health authorities which control budgets, and which are seen to be responsible for the quality of service. Through local authorities which are reformed and reinvigorated to stimulate real popular accountability for their decisions – perhaps via mechanisms such as an elective chief executive. Through the development of systems of industrial democracy which would be – would have to be – eclectic and varied, but which would be statutorily bound to institutionalise consultation and the disclosure of plans and forecasts. Such arrangements would be inclusive of all employees, and thus could not become trade union monopolies or forums for sectional squabbles – though in many plants, the unions would have an important organisational role.

Again, Labour can draw on its traditions to provide a renaissance in public provision from below. For example (the example is Frank Field's) suppose the Jobcentres were to be privatised (no reason why the Government should not think of it). The trade unions had, in the last century, the self-imposed task of collecting vacancies for their members; they could again find a larger role than that to which they have been confined, in managing a service which has been in state hands since the beginning of the century. It would, of course, be a different service – more comprehensive, regulated by government, making no distinctions between members and non-members of trade unions – but why should the TUC not seek financial backing and attempt a bid? Why simply stand on the sidelines while a commercial employment agency takes the job? Why not extend union influence *without* assistance from the state? What a prize if it won! – proof that the collective delivery of common services could be performed and could find public support.

To support these and other new or reformed centres of accountability would be programmes of civic education: a deliberately inclusive and heuristic process whose purpose would be to allow the citizen to be active by making him or her *informed* first. It is false egalitarianism to pretend that all are on an equal footing in the matter of participation and it is a matter of common observation that the civic processes are increasingly monopolised by the well-educated (if not always the intelligent and responsible). It is of no use to bemoan the withdrawal of much of the working class and all of the 'underclass' from public politics. Parties of the left have a responsibility encoded in their ideology, as well as a more urgent vested interest, in reversing the trend, where it *is* a trend, and in creating a new platform for involvement and activity. Such a platform was partially provided by the trade union movement and, in a weaker form, still is: but it is far *too* partial and spasmodic to stand as a proxy for an exercise in citizenship which must be ambitious and energetic.

Underlying this programme – the promotion of an engaged democracy – are assumptions which are explicitly anti-laissez-faire. First, the programme assumes, along with the Government, that there are critical matters in society which require addressing (although it does not assume that a mere turning of the rhetorical tap will perform the trick); second, that a more equal participation in citizenship requires at least that the starting blocks be brought into a closer relationship with each other through education and training; third, and most importantly, that the colossally powerful forces which mass production, consumption and leisure patterns have unleashed and continue to unleash upon social and demographic structures, need the most active intervention in constructing sociable and democratic networks, if we are to prevent much of society, especially in the urban sprawls, drifting into anomie.

The structures on which we have relied are often silted up. It has been the insights and the sharp opportunism of a radical conservatism which has appreciated this, and which has seen that they can be sniped at, damaged, even wholly destroyed without general protest from a public who have felt as much victims of these structures as clients of them – the more so the more 'caring' these structures and services have claimed to be. The political trick has been sharp but has cut both ways – against a left which often occupied the structures and complacently acquiesced in their decreasing effectiveness and accountability – but also, now, against the people who have been given nothing, or nothing efficient, in their place, through which to pursue rights, redress grievances or exercise their political choice.

Few movements have better illuminated the power and value of a really active citizenry than the environmental. For two decades derided as the preserve of the crank (by this writer among others), the movement has in the past two years been entered into the conference halls and committee rooms of power on a wave of panic. The destruction wrought on atmosphere, soil, rivers, forest and ocean and the continuing games of chance we play with our technologies are to remain the central stuff of politics in our times, and probably beyond. That the interlocking crises already evident will require urgent and disinterested international cooperation is clear. They may also require a profound change in consumption levels and expectations if disasters for at least parts of the globe – they are likely to be the already-poorest – are to be averted.

The environmental movement has had the nerve and the skill to dramatise these matters and make them live. It has done so as a purely civil and autonomous development, working through education, dramatisation and persuasion. It is a model for the politics of our time.

At the very least, Labour should have had the conservatism knocked out of it by now. It will be bequeathed a certain political landscape and it has in any case an unfinished or, perhaps better, an unstarted, programme: the building of a new civil order robust enough to elevate popular will to the same level as capital, yet transparent enough to respond to the public will as expressed through elections, polls and the judgement of politicians accountable to an active electorate.

The traditions Conservatism draws on are paternalist or laissez-faire: both are hostile or at least indifferent to collective endeavour and to elective agencies below Parliament. Labour, especially, has different traditions and strengths. It is these which can now be refurbished to meet the new times.

. . . change forthwith the old conditions

The left has not concerned itself excessively with the constitution. Labour Governments in power have not disturbed it. Out of power, the Labour Party has sounded more radical, but it has been under little pressure to act – so a great deal of that has been puff. The monarchy is thought to be beyond reach, the House of Lords to be convenient for patronage and the voting system as apt – until this decade – to return a Labour as a Conservative government. More pressing matters have demanded time – the economy, control of industry, the labour market, civil liberties legislation. Who is to say these priorities are wrong?

Further left, the analysis has been sharper and deeper (if ineffective). The view that Britain's democracy is a flawed and partial one which, by the relative ease of its development and its willingness to compromise, has created neither a thoroughgoing bourgeois class nor a relatively transparent governing structure, has been strongly put and has gained ground. It is fair to say, however, that the main political quest for the far left has been the search for a revolutionary working class, or proxies for it. Constitutional change as part of a reformist programme has not been seen as important or, in itself, desirable.

The political groupings which have been consistently enthusiastic for such a change over time are naturally the parties whose representation in Parliament is nil or much smaller than their popular vote. The Liberal Party has been the most important of these and the most consistent advocate of proportional representation. Its demands were dismissed as self-interested for most of the post-war period. This, however, ceased to be the case in the 1970s and is painfully at odds with voting patterns in the 1980s.

There had been a perfectly good functional argument for the two-party system: it worked to secure stable governments which were accepted as representative throughout the UK (always excepting Northern Ireland, tragically cut out of British political development). Now it does not.

Much is made of Thatcher's 'elective dictatorship'. There is no difference in principle, between the elective dictatorship of previous governments, many of these elected on a minority vote – though of course in practice, the Thatcher Government has been more corrosive. The growth of third and fourth parties and their lack of adequate representation, is the genuine argument for the two-party system. It now seems certain that British politics will *not* revert to a two-party pattern and thus the voting system will continue to be exposed as undemocratic.

There is here a coincidence of interest between the parties of the opposition. The power which the Government has been able to concentrate in its hands has neutered much of that previously held in local government and other devolved centres. The House of Lords, virtually powerless and largely disregarded, except when it can delay or marginally amend legislation, is the more starkly seen as the absurdity it is. The monarchy cannot survive (it is to be hoped) much more of the damage visited upon its dignity by the popular press. It is difficult to imagine Charles able to uphold the royal mummery with the grave decorum of his mother. The cauterising effect of Mrs Thatcher's neo-Liberals has shone a harsher light on the constitution than it has been used to, or that it can bear: an excellent opening for a government of the left to argue for a thorough-going reform.

The platform on which it would stand would be the democratisation and renewal of British public life. The inclusion of the citizenry in the political processes cannot properly be effected while the Commons does not reflect the popular vote, while the Lords has *no* popular vote and while the monarchy hangs over all, bloated and useless. Something of even Thatcher's radicalism and populism has proved infectious. The old game is up: a government of the left cannot come in on a conservative ticket.

Labour must now develop proposals for proportional representation, for an elective second chamber and for a diminution of the role of the monarchy. The last, while symbolically important, is less so than the first two, which need the widest consultation and deepest thought, certainly, but must be done. These reforms also need the deployment of the best talent and energies on the opposition benches. They are a classic cause for politicians to take to the country (or the TV studios) and to proclaim with revivalist force. They will meet genuine conservatism from Labour as well as Conservative and centrist voters, but they present themselves as a tremendous task on which Labour can lead.

Indeed, without such a change, the questions of devolved government to Scotland, and even to English regions, seems premature. If the Scots wish to govern themselves, I can think of no good reason why they should not (though their living standards would be lower). If, as they have always indicated, they wish to stay within the United Kingdom, the important matter of devolution should be part of the wider matter of overall constitutional reform.

Two further issues here. First, the constitutional position of Northern Ireland has been consigned to a tragic limbo. It is time for Labour to take a radical initiative. The Anglo-Irish agreement, on which there is a parliamentary consensus, has not and cannot deliver a 'solution' in either the short or long term since it runs against the grain of what the majority of the Northern Irish want – which is to remain British. This is the true 'Unionist veto': a democratic choice. Yet as long as the people of the province are unable to choose governments because of the failure of the UK parties to offer themselves for election there, the stage is set for undemocratic solutions. Whatever talent and courage successive Northern Irish secretaries have shown, they are ultimately unaccountable to the people they govern.

Since there is no immediate prospect of the majority assenting to union with the Republic, we must recognise majority inclination by granting *all* Northern Irish citizens equal citizenship rights with those of the rest of the UK – that is, being able to vote for the parties which govern them. The discipline of framing platforms which would gain votes in Northern Ireland would not guarantee instant peace, any more than any other 'solution' has. Nor would it rule out future changes in the province's status – any more than Scotland's integration into the rest of the UK presently does. It would however make accountable those who are presently unaccountable.

The second matter is an internal affair of the Labour Party, but one with obvious external consequences. Labour cannot propose fuller democracy in the country while remaining saddled with an undemocratic system of its own. The block vote is composed, in the main, of phantoms who are neither consulted nor allowed to vote individually on the great issues which 'their' votes settle. The unions were the largest element in the Party's founding and are by far its largest pay-masters: but they should now see that none of this gives them the right to a dominance which must rest with individual members, who *are* the Party. The block vote must end, for its maintenance saps the strength out of the Party's democratic projects.

Labour will, however, reinvigorate only part of its mission through an extension of rights and of democracy. Certainly, its concern to erode inequalities and to bring a very large body of people out of poverty and dependence will only secondarily be addressed by these means. Democracy requires another principle: it is best called *reciprocity*. By this I mean that rights conferred imply responsibilities, and that this should inform the relationship between the citizen and the state.

The public sector has been Labour's preserve. Rightly, it has been felt that if Labour cannot get *that* right, its claim to Government is weakened. Widespread industrial action in many of the public sector areas in the 1978/79 'Winter of Discontent', the rundown nature of much provision and service delivery and the use of councils and council services in an overtly political and sectarian way, has badly damaged the confidence people might otherwise have had in Labour doing a decent public job.

There is however a deeper discontent. Labour's provision has been, perhaps inevitably, top-down. Not just because, as is continually and commonly said, it drew on a Fabian tradition which was 'paternalistic', but more because in the 1940s – when Labour put into place a welfare state and, as importantly, a welfare consensus which lasted through changes of government – society lent itself 'naturally' to being treated in large corporate blocs. If social services, medical care, education and housing were to be delivered quickly and in a relatively egalitarian way, then bureaucracies, standards, rules and prohibitions had to govern their provision. We now know that in any such system, the object of the provision is sooner or later treated not as a consumer but as a real or potential nuisance, that the relationship style too often evolves into harassed irritability on one side and irritable supplication on the other.

We also know how acutely the incipient decay in this relationship was spotted by the Government, and how little they have suffered – rather, how much they have gained – from dismantling or thinning many of the institutions first set in place, or greatly amplified, by Labour. Once again, a route back to a better age, achieved simply by putting back together again that which had been blown apart, is not an option. Once again, a counter-version of radicalism is forced upon the opposition.

If the public sector is to be restored and reinvigorated as it should be – then a new *public sector ethos* must be found. In part, this will consist of importing the managerial revolution into the public sector – giving directors and managers real authority by devolving the accountability for sections and tasks upon them and giving them the power of assessment, reward and penalty; making greater use of consultancies and private agencies for specific tasks; more carefully delineating those tasks which are best approached with public sector, and those with market, solutions. Impressionistic evidence suggests that this would mean both less staff in local and other authorities, and higher and more widely differentiated pay. The largest complaint from the clients of the public services, especially those organised by town halls, is lack of responsiveness and of accountability. The effects of commercial competition mean that managers in the private sector strive to address these complaints in order to keep the customer. Public sector managers do not need to keep customers – often do not wish to *see* customers. Since these customers are more often than not the poorest, and since the services provided to them will usually continue to be provided publicly, for only then can they be consistently subsidised, the clients have to have some form of countervailing power against the service providers, to ensure they do their job.

For that, they need both purchasing power and the power of rights. Purchasing power over services can be assisted through a minimum income guarantee augmented by vouchers for public services which we think should remain commonly available to all and highly efficient. The power of rights can be afforded by the imposition on public agencies and service providers of precise targets to which they would have to perform. These targets would be set by the elective authorities: but the real guardians of their fulfilment would be the users of the services.

The aim here, as before, is *transparency*: that the institutions should have a clear set of guidelines and objectives, a clear management and organisational structure, a clear delineation of the problems faced and a clear assessment of what success they have had and what and why failures have been made.

Take the case of education. Let us say that, after consultation with the elective body and the parents of the children at a given school, the staff finds that both its political masters and its customers – the parents – want a more disciplined and academically rigorous environment. Should the staff not strive to provide it? More precisely, should not the object of policy and of reorganisation in this, as in other comparable areas, be to allow the elective body, the customers and the service providers, to each have their areas of authority – but with the bias towards the consumer, who is both paying for the service and, in the case of education, needing it for a richer life?

The example of education illustrates a further necessity. The last decade has seen an attack on the public sector not just because it is inefficient (which it can be) or remote (which it can be), but because it is *public*. Cabinet members who all send their sons and daughters to private schools are likely to have inwardly accepted that the private sector delivers better results and that the public sector is a second class service. And – at least in academic terms – they are right.

Not to seek to redress this imbalance is a terrible perversion of the real, social priorities. Labour in power would have a duty to pick up once again the task of raising standards in the schools to which 90 per cent of the country's children go. More money must be part of that: money for a better-rewarded teaching profession (or where are teachers to come from, especially when competition for graduates intensifies?), for new buildings and equipment. But that money will be wasted unless we give priority to the fullest and most imaginative development of children; unless we acknowledge that only by developing *them* will the country itself raise its productive and cultural level; unless we understand that education does not end in the late teens, but is a constant accompaniment to a full life. Some of these issues are being faced by the Government – they could hardly be wholly ignored – but it is inhibited by its bias towards the private sector and a lack of will or inclination to mobilise the resources and enthusiasm needed to reinvigorate British education. A task, once more, for a party which believes in public provision. But public provision has two sides: the other belongs to us.

. . . arise . . . from your slumbers

The low level of many public services is due to bad providers, but also to bad customers. If we are to make our public sphere better, *we* – as citizens – must make it so.

The development of a public sector ethic based very largely on top-down provision meant that it was careless of cultivating a reciprocal culture in which the customer as well as the provider had certain obligations. Obedience to the regulations was all that was required: a more active relationship would have threatened the bureaucratic structure which, as I've noted, was doing a good enough job according to its lights and did not wish to be disturbed.

We now must have such an active relationship, or the public services will atrophy to the point where they will all *have* to be replaced by market-based services in order to survive in any form. Ensuring transparency from the service providers' side is only part of the matter: on the public side, responsibilities must also be clear.

Thus, in the example above, the school should expect to meet parents who not only take an interest in the form and quality of the education, but who also prepare their children for school in such a way that they are not disruptive to others.

Legislation will have a limited role here: but it must be made explicitly part of a social contract. Public responsiveness must be sought and prepared for, not just given space.

It is in this spirit that Labour must approach the labour market. As this is written, unemployment hovers just below 2 million. It represents a huge mass of poverty and waste, yet it has been hugely encouraging to see more than a million taken off the jobless totals in the past two years.

The drop in the unemployed is both a danger and an opportunity. It is a danger because the fall has meant it is no longer an 'issue' – or, insofar as it is, it rebounds to the credit of the Government. It is an opportunity because it points to a possibility which would have seemed utopian until very recently – the planned creation of full employment.

State intervention in the labour market on the supply side is now a large and accepted part of the political scene. The present Government does more of it than any previous one, and spends more money on the labour market than Sweden – mainly, of course, on subsistence unemployment benefits. Still, such schemes as Youth Training and Employment Training, and the wider and wider spread of these schemes, give rise to the question – why leave anyone out of the 'safety net'? *Why not create full employment?*

It is in the best traditions of the labour movement that it has regarded work as a defining characteristic of full citizenship and that it has – if not always full-heartedly – sought to make it easier for women to return to work after child-bearing. That has to be given much more support by a future government which does not, as this one does, from time to time express a preference for women to retreat into the home and prolonged motherhood. Support means nursery and creche provision at work, adequate maternity and paternity leave and the encouragement of a more equitable division of child care between men and women.

The main object of full employment is a social

one: to allow all citizens to express their needs and creativity, as well as earn their living, in a *social* way, rather than opt out of the social process, which for the poor often means a privatised despair. Labour has always been concerned to raise the living standards of the poor: but it is not enough simply to argue for these living standards to be raised by a little more (it is always in practice a *little* more) on this or that benefit. The poor must be empowered through work – work for which they will often need further training and preparation.

The poor, the marginally employed and the unemployed suffer from an excision from full citizenship; they number many millions. At the same time, it is often said that while as much as thirty per cent of the population may form an 'underclass', the majority enjoy too much comfort and feel too little guilt for any concern to be translated into an electorally popular programme. This may or may not be true, but if it is true, it is only so when put in that way – that is, that the better off must give up income or other goods to raise up the worse off, whom they may regard as undeserving.

Full employment changes that. It will be a difficult objective to achieve: but it is one to which Labour can now commit itself.

Anyone with this aim in view must necessarily contemplate the example of Sweden, the only one of the market economies which has achieved full employment. It has not done so by chance. It has nurtured a consensus that full employment is necessary. It has a vigorous, adaptable and patriotic capitalist sector which has always gone for export-led growth. It has strong formal and informal links between capital, government and labour. It deliberately expanded public sector (generally social service, education and medical) employment in the seventies when industry was restructuring. It has an active labour market policy which intervenes heavily in training. It gives support to industries and workers during restructuring and its further education sector has grown considerably, taking most young people out of the labour market. The main price is, of course, high rates of personal and indirect (though not corporate) taxation.

We cannot become Sweden. Nor should we assume that the network of provision and institutions and reflexes put in place to stop unemployment rising above a residual will also bring about the decline of mass joblessness. But we should also note that some Swedish features – a vigorous capitalism that is willing and able to enter into deals with government and labour, an active training and restructuring policy on the part of the government and the reliance on the public sector to take up those whom industrial change has thrown out of work – are features shared by other successful market economies.

If Labour were to put full employment at the heart of its economic programme, it would need to enlist the committed assistance of capital and organised labour, as well as to substantially expand its own training and educational provisions. More than that: it would have to enter into a myriad of relationships with the voluntary sector – uniquely strong in Britain – encouraging it to draw into full and part-time work very many of those whom employment has passed by for months or years. Within a parliament's lifetime, the aim should be to provide a job or training for all but those temporarily out of work. The potential drawbacks and risks are easy to see – higher taxes, lower productivity, a reversion to bad industrial practices. But those which are unavoidable cannot be worse than the effects of mass unemployment on the men and women who suffer it.

If this were to work, it would need a reciprocal commitment: a responsibility on the part of all to contribute paid work to society, or a willingness to be trained for paid work. When Beveridge drafted his famous report, he envisaged just such a contract. It has never been activated: at first, because it did not seem to be necessary and the trade unions were anyway opposed to it; more recently, because the Government presiding over mass unemployment realised it could do so with relative impunity and did not have the will to provide its side of such a bargain.

To be clear: a government which proposes that everyone who is able to must work or train, or lose all entitlement to unemployment benefit, *can* only do so when it has wrought a great change in the present condition of the labour market. But if it can do so, it is a reasonable – indeed, probably a necessary – bargain. It would be a central element in the creation of a society which is clear about its duties and its rewards.

. . . away with all your superstition

Renewal has been stressed throughout this pamphlet. But it has been at least implicit that there is a need for some sacrifices – some of which are more apparent than real.

Public ownership, somewhat ambiguously sanctioned by Clause 4 of the Party's constitution, acquired great emotional force for three reasons: first, the success of the nationalisation of the coal industry after the war – a success most particularly for miners, whose health, wages and dignity greatly improved; second, the feeling that capitalism is less humane than public ownership, because compelled to make profits; and third, the feeling on the left that nationalisation is an agenda never completed because of cowardly manoeuvring by the right.

The hard pounding suffered by Labour over the last ten years has had the effect of clarifying to a degree the two quite different ways public ownership is seen in the party. It was seen, and is still seen by the left, as a principle: an anti-capitalist mechanism which is always and everywhere superior to the private ownership it replaces. On the other hand, it is also seen as a practical matter: a device for controlling public services which are monopolies or near monopolies and which must have a democratic whip to replace the commercial one.

The second is the only one which can stand serious comparison or scrutiny. Even there, it has to make its case against the alternative mechanisms of control by a regulatory agency, itself accountable to Parliament. Private companies raise increasingly urgent issues of power, of environmental damage, of employment and educational requirements, but since (as I discussed above) they are willy nilly social organisms, they can be further socialised by any government prepared to work with them. It is perfectly clear that states which have preserved social democratic styles of government can also produce successful companies. Indeed, the evidence suggests that the two go together more often than not.

Union power cannot be brought back to the level it occupied in the 1960s and 1970s. I mean that any attempt to make the trade union movement corporately responsible for the country's economic future (especially when it would accept only temporary curbs on free collective bargaining and none on industrial action) is out of the political court.

The huge decline in union power in the past ten years has, of course, been partly the result of political decisions and legislation. It has also been an effect of a rapidly changing labour market – what some commentators have called 'Post-Fordism'. There is no doubt that the smaller, more flexible units of production, the development of a more inclusive managerial style and the strong growth of temporary work have all reduced the scope for trade union organisation.

However, the *representation* of unions is probably too weak in many sectors of the economy – especially where the low paid, women and an over-large proportion of ethnic minorities work. There is no doubt that these workers are exploited and that the exploitation is increased because they do not have a collective voice. Sometimes they are afraid to join a union; sometimes a union has not bothered, or lacks the resources, to organise them. A future government would be concerned to reform in that area. And it would want the unions as a body to develop the internal cohesion (which they do not presently have) to engage in a corporate dialogue with employers (who also lack cohesion).

But it would not want to elevate unions further.

The distancing of the Labour Party from the unions, both through an ending of the block vote and through a clearer definition and hierarchy of roles and responsibilities when in government, does represent a loss. The unions created the Party. They will have to assist in the breaking of many of the bonds. But they must, if the Party is to flourish and take its part in government again.

Unilateralism may pose the largest tactical problem for a Labour leader, but it is the shallowest to uproot. It is not a principle, merely a tactic elevated to one. It has had great moral force behind it, but – in spite of its claims – it has changed little. Change has come from the Soviet Union, which has now declared itself willing to test the West's claim that it has no aggressive designs on the East. At this, most hopeful time, Britain's clear responsibility is to play an active part in all arms reduction forums; to negotiate down, reciprocally and verifiably, the stocks of nuclear weaponry which have consumed so many of the resources, East and West, North and South, which should have been spent on life.

Majority government will be a hard objective to give up, especially for parliamentarians. Shared power clearly brings endless difficulties: a need for deals, for sharing of posts, for the incorporation of different traditions. But majority governments are now only parliamentary creations. There is unlikely to be a *popular* majority for one party for a long time. What is lost in parliamentary coherence is a gain for popular choice.

. . . to win the prize

Much of the process of change, part painful, part exhilarating, is already happening. Labour needs to refashion itself, if it is to be true to the traditions which joined together in its creation, and if it is to serve the political ends for which it is still required.

Refashioned, how much awaits it. It can be

– a party which is again able to command a process of democratic and constitutional change
– a party which can bring a great country's weight behind cooperative and peaceful developments in the world
– a party which can foster and encourage the most generous of our instincts by providing them with material bases and structures
– a party which can give people real power over more of their lives, their futures, and those of their children.

Labour has been at its best when it has expressed the best of the country. It can be so again: there is a *need* that it be so again. Like other parties of the left throughout the world, it has been, and is still, undergoing a series of policy and structural transformations. These are essential, if it is to guide politics in an era of rapid and momentous socio-economic change. Labour has not been, in the past, the most flexible among parties of the left. More than many, it has had difficulty in moving beyond traditional structures and policies which were imbued with the force of scripture.

It has now moved to a position from which it can propose a new politics in a new way. Formerly, it was constrained to *marshal* society into a preordained structure within largely statist institutions; now it seeks to prioritise the popular needs and concerns of the citizenry. It shares in a movement which is becoming common to socialism East and West – a recognition that socialism's future lies in constant interaction with groups and structures of civil society, groups which have autonomous existences but which it is the task of ruling political parties to bring into cooperation. Labour will be able to demonstrate its fitness for that task the better, for being able to cooperate with other parties in taking power from the right in elections, and sharing it, once taken.

The prize is of course political power. However, the job of modern social democracy is not merely to wield power but to disseminate it.

For a decade, Government in Britain has established a certain framework. As it would see it, this is a framework for enterprise, for flexibility and for individual effort, and indeed, it has had some successes in the areas to which it has chosen to give special attention.

But its failures call urgently for a new framework to be set. This would not seek to destroy enterprise. On the contrary, it would seek to enhance and assist it; after all most businesses in this country have some way to go before reaching the levels of the international first rank. But it would also seek to enrich public life by encouraging democratic involvement and cooperative endeavour – by *empowering the citizen*. Labour *knows* there is such a thing as society, but knows too, that society cannot be taken for granted, that it must be nurtured and renewed. In renewing *itself*, Labour is now able to take up that challenge.

About the Author

JOHN LLOYD has worked for newspapers in Edinburgh and London. He has been Labour Editor and Industrial Editor for the *Financial Times*, and Editor of the *New Statesman*. He is former producer of *Weekend World* and *The London Programme*. In 1984 he was voted Journalist of the Year, and he is now Russia correspondent of the *Financial Times*.

CHATTO
CounterBlasts